MIA
HAMM
STRIKING GOLD

JOE LEVIT

LERNER PUBLICATIONS ◆ MINNEAPOLIS

Lerner Publications Company
An imprint of Lerner Publishing Group, Inc.
241 First Avenue North
Minneapolis, MN 55401 USA

For reading levels and more information, look up this title at www.lernerbooks.com.

Main body text set in Myriad Pro Semibold. Typeface provided by Adobe.

Library of Congress Cataloging-in-Publication Data

Names: Levit, Joseph, author.
Title: Mia Hamm / Joe Levit.
Description: Minneapolis : Lerner Publications, [2021] | Series: Epic sports bios (Lerner sports) | Includes bibliographical references and index. | Audience: Ages 7–11 | Audience: Grades 2–3 | Summary: "In 275 career games with the US Women's National Team, soccer superstar Mia Hamm won two Women's World Cup titles and two Olympic gold medals. Learn about the life of US soccer's biggest star"— Provided by publisher.
Identifiers: LCCN 2020015934 (print) | LCCN 2020015935 (ebook) | ISBN 9781728404301 (library binding) | ISBN 9781728420486 (paperback) | ISBN 9781728418087 (ebook)
Subjects: LCSH: Hamm, Mia, 1972-—Juvenile literature. | Women soccer players—United States—Biography—Juvenile literature. | Soccer—United States—Juvenile literature.
Classification: LCC GV942.7.H27 L48 2021 (print) | LCC GV942.7.H27 (ebook) | DDC 796.334092 [B]—dc23

LC record available at https://lccn.loc.gov/2020015934
LC ebook record available at https://lccn.loc.gov/2020015935

Manufactured in the United States of America
1-48488-49002-1/21/2021

TABLE OF CONTENTS

COOL UNDER PRESSURE

The game was deadlocked. Mia Hamm and the United States Women's National Team (USWNT) fought China to a scoreless draw at the 1999 Women's World Cup final. Then the teams battled through two scoreless periods of extra time. The game came down to penalty kicks.

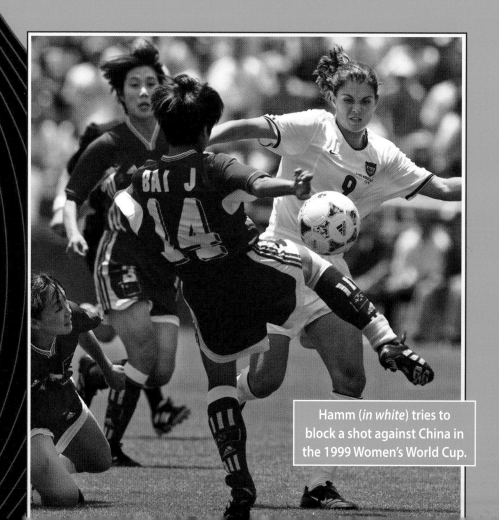

Hamm (*in white*) tries to block a shot against China in the 1999 Women's World Cup.

FACTS AT A GLANCE

Date of birth: March 17, 1972

Position: forward, midfielder

League: USWNT

Professional highlights: won two Women's World Cups and two Olympic gold medals; set a record for most career goals in women's international soccer matches; appeared on the FIFA 100, a list of the 125 greatest living soccer players

Personal highlights: daughter of a US Air Force pilot; spent part of her childhood living in Italy; started the Mia Hamm Foundation

During the penalty kicks, the US goalie made a great save to keep the score tied 2–2. Then the USWNT took the lead on their next kick. But China came right back and tied it with a goal.

China's goalkeeper can't reach the ball as Brandi Chastain scores for the US.

Hamm holds the 1999 Women's World Cup championship trophy.

It was Hamm's turn to kick. She launched the ball past China's goalie for a 4–3 lead. A few moments later, Brandi Chastain scored to win the game for the USWNT. US fans in the stadium erupted in cheers as Hamm and her teammates celebrated.

ALWAYS ON THE MOVE

On March 17, 1972, Mia Hamm was born in Selma, Alabama. From an early age, she loved to play soccer. Her father was a US Air Force pilot, so the Hamm family never stayed in one place for long. Before Mia was two, the family moved to Italy.

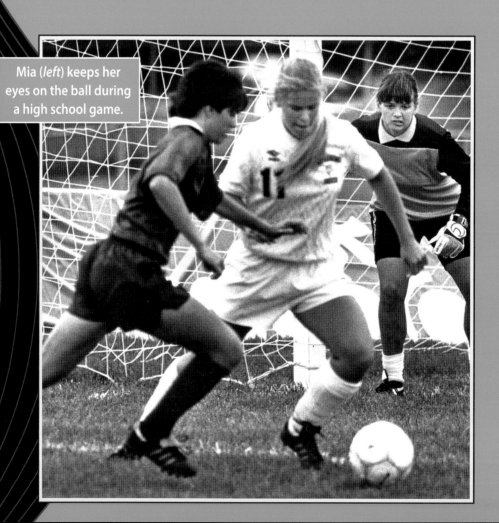

Mia (*left*) keeps her eyes on the ball during a high school game.

Soccer is the most popular sport in Italy.

In Florence, Italy, almost everybody loved soccer. When the national team was on TV, most people stopped what they were doing to watch. Kids all around the city played soccer together. Mia tried to keep up with her older sisters and older brother. She seemed to never stop running.

In 1975, Mia and her family moved to Texas. Her mom wanted her to try ballet. But Mia found it boring, and she didn't like wearing ballet shoes. She wanted to play soccer instead. "Sports was a really good way for me to meet people, an easy way for me to express myself," Mia said.

In 1977, Mia's family adopted an eight-year-old boy named Garrett. Like Mia, Garrett enjoyed sports. He encouraged her to play soccer.

At the age of five, Mia was finally old enough to join a soccer team. Her father was the coach. Mia was smaller than most of her teammates, but she knew how to find open spaces on the field. She gained confidence as she scored goals.

Mia (*right*) plays in an all-star game.

Anson Dorrance is the most successful coach in US women's college soccer.

When Mia was 13 years old, Anson Dorrance saw her in action on a soccer field. Dorrance coached the University of North Carolina (UNC) women's soccer team and the USWNT. Dorrance knew Mia was special right away. As soon as the game started, Dorrance said she "took off like she was shot out of a cannon."

AMATEUR CHAMPIONSHIPS

Mia joined the USWNT in 1987. At 15 years old, she was the youngest player on the team. The USWNT played two matches against China's national team. Mia didn't score a goal, but she had no trouble keeping up with her older teammates.

Mia blasts a shot during practice.

In 1988, Mia's family moved to Virginia. She helped her new high school team win the 1989 soccer state championship. In the fall, she joined the UNC women's soccer team.

The UNC Tar Heels had won three straight national college championships. In the 1989 conference title game, Hamm scored two goals to help her team win. The Tar Heels went on to win the national title that year and the next. In 1990, Mia won the Conference Player of the Year award.

Mia (*center*) worked hard in practice to make the most of her talent.

The 1991 Women's World Cup took place at Tianhe Stadium in Guangzhou, China.

In 1991, China hosted the first Women's World Cup. Hamm wanted to play at the historic event. She left UNC after her second year to play with the USWNT.

The USWNT trained together for months. They played practice matches against other national teams and lost more often than they won. But they learned from their mistakes.

In Hamm's first World Cup game, she kicked the winning goal in a hard-fought 3–2 upset of Sweden. Then Team USA rattled off four straight wins. They faced Norway in the final. Norway had beaten the USWNT twice earlier in the year. But this time, Hamm and her teammates won 2–1 to become world champions.

Hamm raises her arms to embrace her teammates after the USWNT won the first Women's World Cup.

UPS AND DOWNS

After helping Team USA win the 1991 Women's World Cup, Hamm returned to UNC. In a game against the Duke Blue Devils, she had three assists in a 3–1 victory. UNC met Duke again in the 1992 national championship game. This time, Hamm scored three goals in a 9–1 blowout win. The team finished the season 25–0.

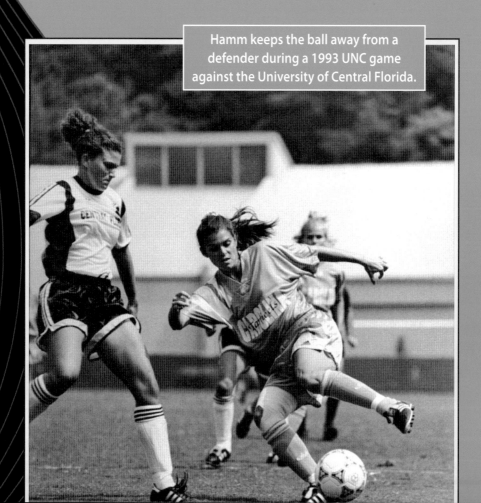

Hamm keeps the ball away from a defender during a 1993 UNC game against the University of Central Florida.

Hamm helped UNC win another championship in 1993. It was her last college season. During Hamm's UNC career, the Tar Heels won four national titles and had an incredible 92–1–2 record.

Sweden hosted the 1995 Women's World Cup. Hamm and the USWNT advanced to the knockout round. They beat Japan by four goals before losing to Norway 1–0.

A defender from Norway trips Hamm during the 1995 Women's World Cup.

Hamm is shadowed by a Swedish player during the USWNT's second match at the 1996 Olympic Games.

Hamm and her teammates were upset by the loss. But the USWNT regrouped quickly and began to prepare for the 1996 Olympic Games in Atlanta, Georgia. For the first time, women's soccer would be an Olympic event. The USWNT lived and practiced together. They were committed to reclaiming their place as the world's top team.

Team USA cruised past Denmark in the Olympic opener 3–0. Then they squeezed by Sweden 2–1. But Hamm injured her ankle against Sweden. She missed the next game.

In the knockout round, Hamm's ankle was still injured. But she played through the pain. "Mia's impact on a game is tremendous even when she isn't 100 percent," said US goalie Briana Scurry.

The gold medal game against China was tied 1–1 after almost 70 minutes. Hamm rushed up the right side of the field and passed the ball to Joy Fawcett in the middle. Fawcett passed to Tiffeny Milbrett, who scored to give Team USA the gold medal.

Tiffeny Milbrett reacts with joy to her goal against Team China.

After the game, Hamm saw her brother Garrett at the team hotel. "He kept telling me how proud he was of me," Hamm said. Garrett had a rare disease and died in April 1997. Hamm later started the Mia Hamm Foundation to help people who have similar diseases. The foundation also supports young women in sports.

EQUAL TREATMENT

Title IX requires US schools to treat students equally regardless of their gender. The law helps female students play soccer, basketball, and other sports. Title IX became law in 1972, the year Hamm was born. The Mia Hamm Foundation supports Title IX and provides money to help female athletes play sports.

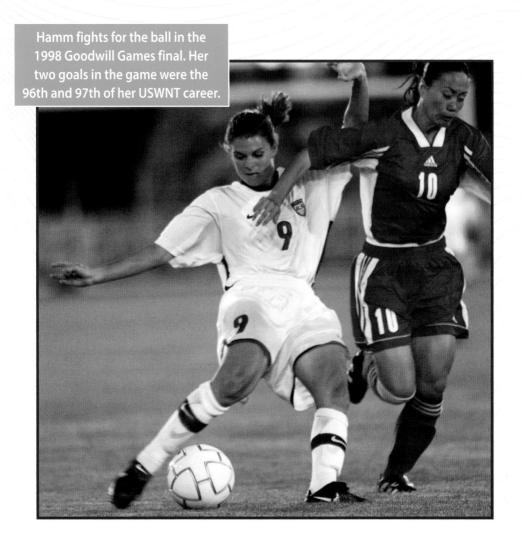

Hamm fights for the ball in the 1998 Goodwill Games final. Her two goals in the game were the 96th and 97th of her USWNT career.

A year later, Hamm helped the USWNT win the Goodwill Games. She scored three goals against Denmark in a 5–0 victory. It was the ninth three-goal game of Hamm's US career. Then she scored both her team's goals in a 2–0 win against China in the final.

GOING FOR GOLD AGAIN

In the 1970s and 1980s, Italy's Elisabetta Vignotto set a record with 107 career goals in women's international matches. In a game against Brazil on May 22, 1999, Hamm beat two defenders to score. It was the 108th goal of her career, breaking Vignotto's record.

Hamm (*center right*) celebrates with her teammates after setting the all-time international scoring record.

Hamm was one of the fastest players on the field at the 1999 Women's World Cup.

The 1999 Women's World Cup was a chance for Hamm and the USWNT to put their 1995 third-place finish behind them. They won all three of their group round matches. In the knockout round, they defeated Germany 3–2. Then they beat Brazil 2–0 in the next match, a game that was much closer than the score showed. In the final, the USWNT took down China for the USWNT's second Women's World Cup title.

The USWNT traveled to Sydney, Australia, for the 2000 Olympics. Leading up to the games, they lost two matches to Norway and tied Brazil. Winning the gold medal would be a tough task.

The US faced Norway first. Hamm scored the second goal of a 2–0 victory. The USWNT tied China before beating Nigeria. In the knockout round, Hamm scored the game's only goal as the US barely scraped by Brazil 1–0. In the final, the USWNT faced Norway again. The teams battled to a 2–2 tie. But in extra time, Norway snatched gold with a goal.

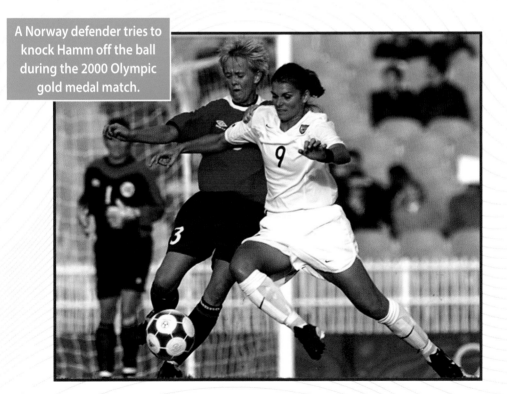

A Norway defender tries to knock Hamm off the ball during the 2000 Olympic gold medal match.

Sweden's goalkeeper dives to stop Hamm from scoring.

The United States hosted the 2003 Women's World Cup. It was Hamm's fourth World Cup, and she was eager to defend the title she helped win in 1999. In the group round, the USWNT beat Sweden 3–1. Hamm assisted all three goals. Then the US beat Nigeria and North Korea to reach the knockout round. The USWNT beat Norway 1–0. But they lost 3–0 to Germany in the next game. The US won bronze by besting Canada 3–1. Hamm wasn't happy with third place. She began preparing for the 2004 Olympics in Athens, Greece.

A SPORTY MATCH

In November 2003, Hamm married Major League Baseball shortstop Nomar Garciaparra. They have twin daughters, Grace Isabella and Ava Caroline. Their son, Garrett Anthony, is named after Hamm's brother.

At the Olympics, the USWNT faced Greece in the first contest. Hamm scored the final goal in a 3–0 victory. The US advanced to the knockout round where they beat Japan and then Germany. In the final, they topped Brazil in a 2–1 thriller to win gold.

Hamm retired after the 2004 Olympics. It's often hard for world-famous athletes to hang up their gear and call it a career. But Hamm was ready. "Will I miss playing soccer?" she said. "Absolutely. But I'm at peace with my decision. It definitely is time to move on with my life."

Hamm and Nomar Garciaparra attend a 2006 charity event in California.

SIGNIFICANT STATS

Led the nation in scoring with UNC in 1990, 1992, and 1993.

Won the women's US Soccer Player of the Year award five straight times (1994–1998).

Won the World Player of the Year award in 2001 and 2002.

Scored her 151st international goal in 2004, the most ever by any player. Her record stood for nine years.

Inducted into the US National Soccer Hall of Fame in 2007.

GLOSSARY

assist: a pass that leads directly to a goal

conference: a group of sports teams that play one another

FIFA: a group that oversees soccer around the world

final: the championship match of a tournament

goal: when a player kicks the ball past a goalie and into the net

group round: the stage of a tournament in which teams in a group play one another. The top two teams usually advance to the knockout round.

knockout round: the stage of a tournament in which a game's winning team advances to the next round and the losing team is out of the tournament

penalty kick: a free kick at the goal allowed for certain fouls or to decide the winner of some games

upset: when a game is won by a team that is expected to lose

SOURCE NOTES

9   Bonnie DeSimone, "Mia Hamm," *Chicago Tribune*, June 18, 1999, https://www.chicagotribune.com/news/ct-xpm-1999-06-18 -9906200412-story.html.

11   Dwight Chapin, "Mia Hamm Is the Reluctant Star of Women's Soccer," SFGate, last modified February 6, 2012, https://www .sfgate.com/sports/article/Mia-Hamm-is-the-reluctant-star-of -women-s-soccer-3079903.php.

19   Michael Farber, "Score One for Women," *Sports Illustrated*, August 12, 1996, https://vault.si.com/vault/1996/08/12/uswnt-1996 -olympics-gold-medal-china-atlanta.

20   Amy Shipley, "A Golden Moment Touched by Sorrow," *Washington Post*, June 8, 1997, https://www.washingtonpost.com/archive /sports/1997/06/08/a-golden-moment-touched-by-sorrow /94633b5f-5ce3-4010-8b08-3318c8e2f6a0/.

27   Scott Pitoniak, "Hamm Will Retire after Olympics," *Spokane Spokesman-Review*, June 29, 2004, https://www.spokesman.com /stories/2004/jun/29/hamm-will-retire-after-olympics/.

LEARN MORE

Mia Hamm
https://www.nationalsoccerhof.com/players/mia-hamm.html

Mia Hamm Foundation
http://www.miafoundation.org/

Scheff, Matt. *The Summer Olympics: World's Best Athletic Competition.*
Minneapolis: Lerner Publications, 2021.

Scheff, Matt. *The World Cup: Soccer's Greatest Tournament.*
Minneapolis: Lerner Publications, 2021.

Skinner, J. E. *U.S. Women's National Soccer Team.* Ann Arbor, MI:
Cherry Lake, 2019.

U.S. Women's National Team
https://www.ussoccer.com/teams/uswnt

INDEX

PHOTO ACKNOWLEDGMENTS

Image credits: Michael Caulfield/Photographer, p. 4; Todd Strand/Independent Picture Service, pp. 5, 28; Mark J. Terrill/Photographer, p. 6; © Globe Photos/ZUMAPRESS.com/ Alamy Stock Photo, p. 7; John R. Van Beekum/The Washington Post/Getty Images, p. 8; Tuangtong Soraprasert/Shutterstock.com, p. 9; Getty Images Sport/Getty Images, p. 10; AP Photo/Icon Sportswire, p. 11; Will Mcintyre/The LIFE Images Collection/Getty Images, pp. 12, 13, 16; © Alexchen4836 via Wikicommons (CC BY-SA 3.0), p. 14; Bob Thomas/Getty Images, p. 15; Rick Stewart/Allsport/Getty Images, p. 17; AP Photo/Chris O'Meara, p. 18; AP Photo/Joe Cavaretta, p. 19; AP Photo/Ron Frehm, p. 21; AP Photo/Scott Audette, p. 22; AP Photo/John T. Greilick, p. 23; AP Photo/Tony Gutierrez, p. 24; AP Photo/Lawrence Jackson, p. 25; AP Photo/Branimir Kvartuc, p. 27.

Cover images: tony quinn/Alamy Stock Photo; AP Photo/John Biever.